The History of the Order of the Eastern Star Among Colored People

Also from Westphalia Press
westphaliapress.org

The History of the Order of the Eastern Star Among Colored People

by Mrs. S. Joe Brown

WESTPHALIA PRESS
An Imprint of Policy Studies Organization

Westphalia Press
An imprint of Policy Studies Organization
1527 New Hampshire Ave., NW
Washington, D.C. 20036
info@ipsonet.org

ISBN-13: 978-1-63391-562-6
ISBN-10: -63391-562-X

Cover design by Jeffrey Barnes:
jbarnesbook.design

Daniel Gutierrez-Sandoval, Executive Director
PSO and Westphalia Press

Updated material and comments on this edition
can be found at the Westphalia Press website:
www.westphaliapress.org

THIS HISTORY OF O.E.S. AMONG COLORED
PEOPLE

is

FRATERNALLY DEDICATED

By the Author to her Co-laborers, and those
Sainted pioneers who have made possible

this Record

MRS. S. JOE BROWN

THE HISTORY

OF THE

ORDER OF THE EASTERN STAR
AMONG COLORED PEOPLE

BY

MRS. S. JOE BROWN
MATRON OF THE INTERNATIONAL
CONFERENCE OF GRAND CHAPTERS
OF O.E.S.

Illustrated

Publilshed at Des Moines, Iowa
March, 1925

CONTENTS

FOREWORD

After associating, in a fraternal way, With Sister S. Joe Brown, of Des Moines, Iowa, our International Grand Matron, and having sat and listened attentively to her reading at Pittsburgh, Pa., Aug. 19, 1924, I am firmly of the opinion that Sister Brown, in the accompanying work, has given to the Eastern Star world the result of years of study, travel and research, which in my judgment, is the most complete concise and authentic history of the Order, among our group of any yet presented. It has rightfully been adopted by the International Conference of Grand Chapters as the official history of the Order and all Grand Chapters should accept it and see that it is properly distributed throughout its bounds, as a long desired necessity.

Sister Brown, in giving this history to the Eastern Star world, has no doubt, added more to our universal understanding and unification than any other one agency, and it will redound to her honor and glorification in years to come.

Our prayer is that she may retain her health and youthfulness and for many years to come, adorn and serve the race and Order. We bespeak for this volume ready acceptance and a broad circulation, throughout the Grand Chapters.

J. C. SCOTT,
International Grand Patron

PREFACE

In compliance with a recommendation made in
our report to the Ninth Biennial Session of our International Conference of Grand Chapters of the
Order of the Eastern Star, that a committee be
appointed to publish a brief History of our Order,
and out of consideration for the detailed report
submitted at this session, the Conference voted to
have published said report as the official History
of the Order as expressed in the "Foreword" by
Bro. J. C. Scott of Texas, who has not only served
in that Jurisdiction as Grand Patron the past 30
years, but who also serves as Patron in our International Conference; it is however, with a bit of
timidity that I reproduce the report as made at
the Conference but by authority of said conference
I do this, and in addition thereto I herewith sub-
mit other data gathered from various sources from
the several Jurisdictions, and otherwise, as a
result of which there will be found in this little
volume a list of the Jurisdictions for the most part
the year and the date of organization, time of
annual meeting, tabulated statistics showing number of Chapters and number of members of each
Jurisdiction, Grand Matron and Grand Patron serving in 1924 in the United States of America, in
Ontario, Canada, and in Liberia, Africa. And by
the way of showing some of the most tangible
achievements of our Order we also present a few Il-
lustrations such as Widows' and Orphans' Homes,
Temples, etc., and a historical sketch of each tell-
ing of the part the Order has played in the erec-
tion and maintenance of each.

THE AUTHOR

PRINCE HALL, Founder of Negro Masonry

1784
THE ORIGINAL CHARTER

(Copy)

Know all men by these presents:

Thus were we greeted by the Grand Lodge on the 29th day of September, A.L. 5784, A.D.1784; and following said Greeting was warrant 459, granted by the Grand Lodge of England, on petition of Prince Hall, Boston Smith, Thomas Sanderson, and several other Masons of Boston, constituting them into a regular Lodge of Free and Accepted Masons.

"To all and every right Worshipful and loving Bretheren we, Thomas Howard, Earl of Effingham, Lord Howard, etc., etc., acting Grand Master under the authority cf His Royal Highness, Henry Frederick, Duke of Cumberland, etc., etc., Grand Master of the Most Ancient and Honorable Society of Free and Accepted Masons send Greeting:

"Know ye, that we, at the humble petition of our right trusty and well beloved Brethren, Prince Hall, Boston Smith, Thomas Sanderson and several other Brethren residing in Boston, New England, in North America, do hereby constitute the said Brethren into a regular Lodge of Free and Accepted Masons, under the title or denomination of the Afrcan Lodge to be opened in Boston aforesaid, and do further, at their said petition, hereby appoint the said Prince Hall to be a Master, Boston Smith, Senior Warden, and Thomas Sanderson, Junior Warden, for the opening of the said Lodge, and for such further time only as shall be thought proper by the brethren thereof, it being our will that this, our appointment of the above officers, shall in no wise affect any future election of officers of the Lodge, but that such election shall be regulated agreeable to such by-laws of said Lodge as shall be consistent with the general laws of the society contained in the Book of Constitutions, and we hereby will require you, the said Prince Hall, to take especial care that all and every one of the said Brethren are or have been regularly made Masons, and that they do observe, perform and keep all the rules and orders contained in the Book of Constitutions; and further, that you do, from time to time, cause to be entered in a book kept for the purpose, an account of your proceedings in the Lodge, together with all such rules, orders and regulations, as shall be made for the good government of the same; that in no wise you omit once in every year to send us, or our successor, Grand Master, or to Rowland Holt, Esq., our Deputy Grand Master for the time being, an account in writing of your said proceedings, and copies of all such rules, orders and regulations as shall be made as aforesaid, together with a list of the members of the Lodge, and such a sum of money as may suit the circumstances of the Lodge and reasonably be expected towards the Grand Charity. Moreover, we hereby will and require you, the said Prince Hall, as soon as conveniently may be, to send an account in writing of what may be done by virtue of these presents.

"Given at London, under our hand and seal of Masonry, this 29th day of September, A.L., 5784, A.D. 1784.

"By the Grand Master's Command.

SEAL

Witness: "Wm. White, G.S." "R. Holt, D.G.M."

"We, their descendants not only in a Masonic point of view, but in blood as well, standing upon the soil on which they were born, and viewing their play grounds, shall visit the grave of Prince Hall and place our sprig of Acacia thereon.

"Thomas Thomas, G.M., of Masachusetts."

ORIGIN AND HISTORY OF THE ADOPTIVE
RITE IN THE DIST. OF COLUMBIA,

The following is an extract from the Annual Address of Grand Patron Thornton A. Jackson, (33rd degree), delivered at the Second Annual Communication of the Grand   Chapter of the District of Columbia and Jurisdiction, on May 23, 1893, which contains an account of the Histroy and Origin of the Adoptive Rite in the District of Columbia. It is republished here for the information of the members of this Order."

At the organization of this Grand Chapter, I informed you that the history and origin of the Eastern Star Degrees in this Juirsdiction would be of some importance to the members of this Grand Chapter and   Subordinates. I said that our origin was pure and undisputed. I informed you that on the 10th day of August, 1874, I received the several degrees of the Rite of Adoption, of the Order of the Eastern Star, from Bro. C. B. Case, a Deputy and Agent of Illustrious Robert Maccy, (33rd degree), the Supreme   Patron of the Rite of Adoption of the   World, and at   which time I received from Bro. C. B. Case a letter of   authority empowering me to establish this Order among our people. I at cnce proceeded to establish chapters of the Eastren Star in obedience to the authority with which I was invested."

In 1875 and 1876, I established two (2) Chapters at Washington, D. C.; one (1) at Alexandria;in the State cf Virginia; three (3) at Baltimore, in the State of Maryland; and three (at Philadelphia, in the State of Pennsylvania. So you see in the short space of eighteen   months we had nine (9) Chapters of the Order, all in a fair working condition. Notwithstanding my authority to establish the Rite, but like the Grand Orient of France, I had each Chapter   thus   organized, adopted by scme regular constituted Masonic Lodge, thereby more closely uniting our Masonic family. These Chapters, like some of cur Masonic Lodges, for a time seemed to carry all before   them; so they flourished, but soon their course was run, and to-day, out of the the nine (9), all but two (2), Queen

Esther, No. 1 of Washington, D. C., and Electa, No. 2, of Baltimore, Maryland, is a thing of the past.

Two years ago I established at Washington, D. C., Queen of Sheba and Gethsemane Chapters, and authorized Bro. J. Murry Ralph, of Baltimore, Maryland, to establish at Frederick City Maryland, Queen Esther, and at Baltimore, Maryland, Queen of Sheba Chapters, and according to my former instructions each Chapter has been adopted by a regular Masonic Lodge. Now we have a Grand Chapter with six (6) Subordinates, all in a flourishing condition. We are now an independent body."

MASONIC AND O.E.S. HOME—Marion, Ind.

HISTORY OF THE O.E.S. AMONG COLORED PEOPLE

In the city of Boston, in the year 1907, an organization styled as a Supreme Grand Chapter of the O.E.S. was formed by a limited number of representatives of our then existing Grand Chapters that felt the need of a closer fraternal relationship, whereby there might be brought about a better interpretation of and more uniformity in the ritualistic work, and in the end to encourage the organization of Chapters, that they might cooperate in the great labors of Masonry, by assisting in and in some respects directing the charities and other work in the cause of human progress.

Mrs. Letitia L. Foy, then of Massachusetts, but now of Newburn, N. C. called this meeting together at the conclusion of which the following officers were elected:

Supreme Grand Royal Matron, Sister Kittie Terrell of the Illinois Jurisdiction; Supreme Grand Royal Patron, Bro. Walden Banks, New England Jurisdiction; Supreme Associate Matron, Sister Viola Hart, Georgia Jurisdiction; Supreme Grand Treasurer, Sister Addie Duffin, Maryland Jurisdiction.

August 21st and 22nd, 1908 the second meeting of this body was held in Chicago, Ill. with fifteen Jurisdictions represented. At this meeting a Constitution and By-Laws Committee appointed at the previous session, reported a constitution and by-laws which were adopted and a collection for stationery in the sum of $3.57 seems to comprise the entire receipts of this session.

August 23—25, 1910 the third session was held at Detriot, Michigan, with eleven Jurisdictions represented. Among the recommendations made at this meeting were: the printing of a ritual; the change of the name from Supreme Grand Chapter to Inter-state Conference of Grand Chapters; and, the fixing of the time of meeting as biennially, and at the same time and place as the International Conference of Knights Templar; also that each Jurisdiction be required to pay a membership fee of two cents per capita and a total of $54 was collected at this meeting.

August 21—22, 1912 the fourth session was held in Washington, D. C., with eleven Jurisdictions again represented and "The Order of the Eastern Star and its development among our People" was a much discussed topic at this meeting after which a committee was appointed to draft a new Constitution and By-Laws consisting of Hon. Lady Mary Parker, District of Columbia, chairman; Hon. Lady M. D. Hillard, Ohio, Hon. Lady M. L. Freeman, Ky.; Hon. Lady Kittie Terrell, Illinois Jurisdiction; Sir F. J. Richards, Michigan; Sir W. H. Jernagin, Okla.; Hon. Lady Letitia L. Foy, Mass.; and Sir Wm. A. Baltimore, of Dist. of Columbia. The total receipts of this meeting were $60.58.

August 4—6, 1914, the fifth session was held in Pittsburgh, Pa. with twelve Jurisdictions represented. The report of the Constitution and By-Laws Committee was submitted and adopted. The total receipts were $61.61.

August 23—26, 1916, the sixth session was held in Chicago, with eighteen jurisdictions represented "Uniformitory of the work" was the chief topic of discussion and a committee appointed to make research and recommendation upon this subject at the next session. The receipts of this session were $144.33.

The next session was to have been held in Kansas City in 1918 but on account of the World War it was called off.

August 23—26, 1920, the seventh session was held in Cincinnati, Ohio, with twenty jurisdictions represented; but a gloom overshadowed this meeting because of the fact that the Inter-state Matron, Miss Janie L. Cox of the District of Columbia, had passed away just one month prior to the convening of the session. After appropriate memorial service was held in her honor, the principal business of this session was the receiving of the re-

port of the special committee on "Uniformity of
the Work" appointed four years previous,   which
report was as follows:

Cincinnati, Ohio, August 24, 1920.

Royal Grand Matron, Royal Grand Patron, and
Representatives here assembled:—Your committee
to whom was referred four years ago, the subject,
"The Unification of the Ritualistic Work of the
several Jurisdictions of our Affiliation," beg to offer the following as a basis cf general agreement:

After studying the whole system of degrees and
conferring with others, including the successors
of Robert Macoy, who was the successor of Robt.
Morris, author and founder of the Order   of the
Eastern Star, we have agreed that the author and
owner of the works and copyrights, should, ought
to and does know his intentions therein better than
those who would traduce him, and violate their
obligations by injecting innovations into or a sub-
stitute for his works.

1. There is, we   believe,   nothing in ritualism,
more beautiful,   attractive   and edifying,   when
properly handled, than the Amaranth degree; but
before it was written by Robt. Macoy, finishing it
upon his death bed, as a reward for merit for those
who have become proficient in the other degrees,
there was the Eastern Star, complete in its system
of units, harmonious in its construction, beautiful
in sentiment, definite in its teachings of unadul-
terated Christianity, with the birth, life's work,
death, resurrection and ascension of   Christ   our
Redeemer as its fundamental principle.

2.   Though written or published in 1912,   no-
where in it does Alonzo J. Burton, in his history
mention the Amaranth as a working or business
degree.

3. A letter dated August 7, 1920, written by Mr.
J. W. Robertson of the Macoy Publishing Co. reads
as follows:

New York, N. Y., August 7, 1920

Mr. J. C. Scott
    407½ Ninth St., Ft. Worth, Texas
Dear Sir and Bro:—
    We regret to inform you that Mr. John Barker departed this life between fifteen and twenty years ago, and we have no means of knowing what his answer to your question would be.

In this section of the country the Eastern Star and Amaranth are usually separate organizations, having separate Grand Bodies, although one must be a member of the O.E.S. before being granted membership in the Amaranth, and we believe that the writers of the Rituals, and founders of the two Orders, intended the Amaranth to bear the same relation to the O.E.S. that the Royal Arch Chapter bears to the Blue Lodge.

However, this is only our opinion in the matter and would not presume to advise you concerning it. It is without doubt a question that only your Grand Chapters can legally settle.

Fraternally yours,
The Macoy Publishing & Masonic Supply Co.,

J. W. Robertson, Per M. D. L."

4. Less than fifty per cent of our members have the Amaranth degree, which under our present system would be either taxed without representation or denied admittance.

We, therefore, recommend that this body work in the Eastern Star degree, transacting its business therein, and use its intelligent influence to induce all Jurisdictions to do the same, encouraging the growth and spread of the Amaranth as an appendant to the Eastern Star.

We also recommend that Macoy Ritual be our recognized standard of work; that Mackey's Jurisprudence be our legal guide and that Grimke's History our official history."

Respectfully submitted,
J. C. Scott, Chairman
Wm. A. Baltimore
Inez T. Alston

MASONIC ORPHANAGE—Americus, Ga.

This report was unanimously adopted; and another committee to revise the constitution and By-laws appointed consisting of J. C. Scott, Chairman; M. D. Hillard, Sue M. Brown; Inez T. Alston and Louisa U. Webb.

August 7—10, 1922, eighth session was held at Washington, D. C., with twenty-one jurisdictions represented; and amount of money reported at this session $457.58, among the recommendations made at this meeting were "That the Grand Secretary of each jurisdiction affiliated with the Conference be requested to send to the Interstate Secretary immediately after the close of its Annual Communication, the names and addresses of the Grand Matron, Grand Patron, Grand Secretary and Chairman of Committee on Foreign Correspondence.

The Interstate Matron, Mrs. Florence E. Scott also suggested a conference with the Grand Masters for the purpose of discussing the regularity of the action of certain Grand Masters in suspending lodges or members of lodges of A.F. & A.M. for affiliating with Chapters or Grand Chapters of O.E.S. which she contended was impeding the progress of the O.E.S. in several jurisdictions.

Mrs. Louise U. Webb, Interstate Lecturer at this session made the following recommendations:

1. The Order of the Eastern Star or Adoptive Rite, stands alone in its beauty and splendor and should be entirely separate from all other orders having degrees as set forth in "Our Landmark" and by Robt. Morris, the founder of the work. If we as members of the Order of the Eastern Star study and practice this work thoroughly and become proficient in demonstrating it, as it should be, there is enough beauty in its ceremonies, without adding or connecting it with any other order, and too, we are working contrary to the wishes of Macoy, who separated the work in his first ritual and caused the Amaranth Degree to be established as an order known as the Independent Amaranth Court. I therefore, recommend that we separate the Amaranth Court entirely from the Adopted Rite.

2. I recommend that all members of the Eastern Star in attendance at our session be properly re-

galed according to the regalia worn by the members of the Order of the Eastern Star. All worthy Matrons, Past and Present should wear the purple sash three inches wide with gold fringe and emblems of the Order if desired and should be worn from the left shoulder to the right side. The Present and Past Worthy Patrons are entitled to wear the same. The other members in attendance should wear the Eastern Star sash, with the five colors, and should be worn from the right shoulder to the left side, the color blue next to the face. The Star officers should wear the color of sash their point represents. This regulation should be practiced in all Subordinate Chapters to cause a better appearance and have the uniformity of Regalia.

I recommend that a committee be appointed at the next Biennial Session to compile a Ritual with the many important items and ceremonies which is not included in the Macoy Ritual.

3. In conclusion I therefore recommend that the Inter-state Conference approve of the important impressive Eastern Star ceremonies as recommended in the "Book of Instructions' for subordinate Chapters, used by the state of Illinois and compiled by Grand Lecturer of the Inter-state Conference of Grand Chapters, and the same be recommended for the use of Subordinate Chapters included in the jurisdictions affiliated in the Interstate Conference of Grand Chapters of the Order of the Eastern Star.

August 19—22, 1924, the ninth session was held at Pittsburgh, Pa., with thirty-two jurisdictions represented; and the amount of money reported at this session was $558.70.

One of the features of the meeting was a symposium on "Co-operation betwen the A.F. & A.M. and the O.E.S.," the principal speakers being Judge Crittenden; E. Clark, Past Grand Master of Missouri; Atty. S. Joe Brown, Past Grand Master of Iowa; Prof. E. J. Hawkins, Past Grand Master of Kansas and Atty. James E. White of Chicago, attorney for the Imperial Council of N.O.M.S.; Mesdames Lillie Talliaferro, Grand Matron of Okla.; Mary F. Woods, Past Grand Matron of Missouri;

MASONIC TEMPLE— Boley, Okla.

Rosa J. Richardson, Past Grand Matron of Maryland; Etta Hawkins, Grand Matron of Washington and Alice J. Campbell, Grand Matron of New York.

Brother Wm. A. Baltimore of Wasington, D. C., the International Patron, being compelled by illness of his mother to absent himself from the session, for the first time sent the following letter of regret: __

Washington, D. C., August 17, 1924

Mrs. S. Joe Brown
International Grand Matron
Order of the Eastern Star
My dear Sister:

I regret very much to have to state to you that it will not not be possible for me to be present at this conference of Grand Chapters. This will be the first session that I have missed since the organization. But my mother is very sick, and acting upon the advice of her physician, Dr. T. Edward Jones, I shall be compelled to remain near her.

Kindly express my regrets to the Conference and assure the members that I am deeply intrested in the instructive program that has been arranged, and sorry beyond expression that the above circurstances make it impossible for me to be with you on this occasion.

I trust and believe that you will have a very successful session and that all discussions and actions will redound the best interest of all of the Chapters represented in the Conference.

With best wishes for a harmonious, well representative session, and with kindest regards to you and all members, I remain,

Fraternally yours,
Wm. A. Baltimore
International Patron

The "Book of Instructions" recommended at the previous meeting was approved at this session; and the Biennial Address of the International Grand Matron, because of its historic value, was ordered published and the same be used as the official history of the O.E.S. among colored people.

ADDRESS

Delivered by
Mrs. S. Joe Brown
Before Ninth Biennial Conference

Two years ago at our Nation's Capitol, when I received at your hands elevation to this, the highest office within your organization, I felt that I owed you a debt of gratitude, that could be paid only in services to the cause we represent; and the thought most prevalent in my mind was the devising of plans whereby we could make this our 9th Biennial Conference the best in the history of our organization.

Just ten years ago, our International Conference convened in this, the historic City of Pittsburgh with about thirty-nine representatives of about twelve Grand Jurisdictions; and I am sure that the good citizens of Pittsburgh as well as the representatives of the various Jurisdictions who have come here at a sacrifice to both themselves and their Grand Chapters will be eager to note what progress our organization has made during this decade.

First of all permit me to say that anticipating this situation and in order that I might be the better prepared to give out information in response to the frequent inquiries that I was sure I should receive from time to time, in my efforts to inspire those Grand Jurisdictions that had never been represented in our conference as well as to reclaim if possible those that had once been represented but had fallen by the wayside, I attempted to gather all the information possible with reference to the origin and history of the O.E.S. among Colored people in America and elsewhere.

I have found that there was a published record of the Order among white Americans from the year 1857 when Robt. Morris, its founder published his first Ritual down to 1912.

I have also found that there is a published record of Free Masonry among Colored Men of North

America from the institution of the first Lodge under Prince Hall in 1775, down to 1903 but find no mention   whatever of the O.E.S. or any other department of female Masonry among our women.

I therefore began a research among those that I thought might be able to furnish me with such information and having failed to find a compiled record or history of the Order, I proceeded to send out questionnaires seeking such information from the thirty-four   Grand Chapters in the   United States and Canada reputed to be regular; and also made several attempts to ascertain whether there was a Grand Chapter on the Continent of Africa, and the following communication will disclose our finding:

Monrovia, Liberia, August 25, 1924
Mrs. S. Joe Brown,
Interational Grand Matron, O.E.S.,
Des Moines, Iowa, U.S.A.

Dear Sister:—

Your communication inviting us to the International Conference of Grand Chapters O.E.S. which would convene in Pittsburgh, Pa., August 17th, was duly received. But as it was not possible to send a delegate, the Committee was instructed to send a communication immediately. We regret very much that in consequence of some mis-adventure the letter   was not sent, much to the disappointment of our General Grand Matron. However, I am instructed by the G. G. Matron, Mrs. Izetta C. Stevens to write to you, expressing the   warm appreciation of herself and the G. G. Chapter to you for the sisterly interest you take in our Chapter.

I am instructed to say to you that the General Grand Chapter will be glad to have recognition in the International Conference and sincerely regrets the lateness of this writing. If you will kindly keep us informed as to the next conference the Grand Chapter will be pleased to be represented there.

We thank you for your kindly interest and hope
that we will hereafter always be in touch with the
Order of the Eastern Star over there.

Fraternally yours,

for the Grand Chapter,
Sarah R. Freeman
General Grand Secretary.

While en route to Vancouver, B.C., to visit the
Tacoma Grand Chapter of the state of Wash., in its
10th Annual Communication; I was awaiting at
Seattle the arrival of the Grand Matron Mrs. Etta
Hawkins and Grand Patron W. F. Williams of the
Jurisdiction and was approached by a lady of the
other race, who recognizing my O.E.S. emblem in-
quired of my identity and my mission; and upon
being informed that she was from Ketchikan, Alaska, and lived neighbor to a matron of the O.E.S.
whom she was sure would be pleased to have me
pay a visit and furnished me with her name and
address; and I presuming of course that the matron referred to was a member of my own race, being elated over the fact that I had discovered that
we had Chapters and perhaps Grand Chapters in
the far away territory of Alaska, opened correspondence with her only to find that she, like my in-
formant, was a member of the other race, affiliated
with their Grand Chapter as the following letter
will disclose:

Ketchikan, Alaska, November 12, 1923

Mrs. S. Joe Brown,

1058 5th St., Des Moines, Iowa

Dear Sister:—

I am in receipt of a letter written by you
to Mrs. Blackmor, a Past Worthy Matron of our
Chapter asking for the address of our Worthy
Grand Matron.

We, and I think all the Alaska Chapters, are
under the jurisdiction of the General Grand Chapter, and our Most Worthy Grand Matron is, as you
doubtless know, Mrs. Clara R. Franz, 700 Laura
Street, Jacksonville, Fla.

Fraternally yours,

Mrs. C. M. Van Marter, W.M.

EASTERN STAR   ORPHAN HOME—
Ft. Worth Texas

On this trip to the Pacific Coast I travelled nearly five thousand miles, passing thru fourteen different states stopping first in Minnesota, where I visited my own, Electa Grand Chapter of Iowa, and Jurisdiction, which includes a portion of Minnesota and which was holding in St. Paul its 16th Annual Communication in Union Hall.

Finding that I was going to arrive in California the 3rd oldest Grand Chapter, too late for their Annual Communication, I wired them a word of greeting and an invitation to join our International Conference, and upon my arrival at Bakersfield, had a pleasant visit at the home of sister Aline Hueston, G.M., who resides in that city and accompanied me to Los Angeles to a platform meeting on Sunday afternoon, where there appeared upon the same program aside from your International Matron, the Grand Matron of Calif., the Grand Matron of Arizona and a Grand Representative of Colorado. Later in the week the Grand Patron of California, who resides in Los Angeles, arranged a joint meeting between the three subordinate Chapters of that city in the beautiful Masonic Temple which is the property of Negro Masons, where we again appeared on a program with the Grand Patron, two Past Grand Matrons, a Past Grand Master of the California Jurisdiction and the Grand Secretary of the New England Grand Chapter, who like myself was visiting the Golden West.

In Arizona where we made our next stop and which is one of our youngest Grand Jurisdictions, a meeting had been arragned in Phoenix, by the Grand Patron, Bro. Clay Credille, who had been advised of our coming by Sister Lynn Ross Carter, Grand Matron and where we were very pleasantly entertained.

We next found ourselves in the Lone Star State, presided over by our Associate International Patron, Bro. J. C. Scott, whose Grand Communication we also missed by one week. However, thru the courtesy of Brother Scott, we were permitted to visit the Widows and Orphans' Home, the pride of the Texas. O. E.S., and also the magnificant Masonic Temple, the pride of the Texas A.F. & A.M., both located at Ft Worth, and in the latter of which we found the office of our official organ the "Eastern Star."

Our next and last stop was in the "show me" state where we found at St. Louis, the Grand Matron of the United Grand Chapter as well as the Grand Matron of Harmony Grand Chapter, also Princess Fannie G. W. McDonald, Captain of the International Conference of Heroines of the Temple Crusades, in whose home we spent a very pleasant evening after a conference with some of the other outstanding characters of this Jurisdiction.

From St. Louis we returned home, but about two weeks later made a trip to Kansas City, Kansas, where we appeared before the Fourteenth Annual Session of the National Association for the Advancement of Colored People and there met and conferred with the Grand Matron of the Kansas Jurisdiction, which is the only Jurisdiction so far as I am advised that publishes its own Ritual.

Enroute to this Ninth Biennial Conference it was our privilege to visit the 35th Annual Session of the Illinois Grand Chapter which was convening in Chicago the week of August the 12th and presided over by Mrs. Carrie Lee Hamilton, this jurisdiction that gave to us our first Grand Matron of this Conference, we found them holding their meeting in Union Masonic Hall of that city the property of the Masonic Fraternity.

Now as a result of this tour of visitation, gathering data whenever and wherever possible, together with the information that I have received by way of responses to the questionnaires, I have been able to gather and now bring to you the following historical data:

About a half century ago, and just one hundred years after the founding of the first Lodge of Negro A.F. & A.M., Bro. Thornton A. Jackson, having received the degrees from a deputy of Robert Maccy, in the year 1875 instituted in the City of Washington, in the District of Columbia, the frst subordinate Chapter of O.E.S. as will be found in this volume on page fifteen under the Caption History and Origin of the Adoptie Rite in the District of Columbia.

Just five years later, in the year 1880, in the City of Washington, N. C., Bishop J. W. Hood, organized the first Negro Grand Chapter of O.E.S. followed closely by Tennessee in the year of 1881.

Then came California and others in succession until Grand Chapters of O.E.S. have been organized and now exist among Negroes in thirty-five Jurisdictions including that of Ontario, Canada and Liberia, Africa, each of which is supreme within itself and adopts its own form of ritualistic work, which has naturally resulted in a great variety in the manners of working in the varioius Grand Jurisdictions.

After some years there arose a sentiment in favor of closer union and greater uniformity of work among the several Grand Chapters which sentiment doubtless was in the mind of Mother Letitia L. Foy, whom we all love to honor, when in the year 1907 she called together in the historic old City of Boston, representatives of a number of Grand Jurisdictions and formed this organization that is now known as the International Conference of Grand Chapters of O.E.S.

Today we have in our thirty-five Grand Jurisdictions about three thousand five hundred Chapters with more than a hundred thousand members, having in their combined treasuries about a half million dollars. Aside from many of our subordinate Chapters owning property a number of our Grand Chapters are assisting the A.F. & A.M. in maintaining Masonic Temples valued all the way from seven thousand, to six hundred and fifty thousand dollars.

Many others operate Burial Funds and Endowment Departments which pay upon the death of a member from twenty-five to five hundred dollars. Some have their own printing establishments from which their official journals and other publications are issued; and several have their juvenile Department through which the youth of our fraternity are given burial benefits as well as valuable training in the conduct of business and social affairs.

Now while you are to be commended upon the wonderful progress you have made during these forty-nine years of your existence, I am sure you will agree with me that the Order of the Eastern Star, one of the outstanding factors in the world's progress, should be a greater force in stimulating its members to a more intelligent participation in civic, national and international affairs, each standing out in our several communities for a practical application of the principles and ideals exemplified in the characters of our five Heroines.

While as I have already stated a great work is being done in some of our Jurisdictions among the youth of our fraternity; yet realizing as I do that there are many Jurisdictions that have not such a department and that the boys and girls of today are to be the men and women of tomorrow and that upon us rests the grave responsibility of shaping the lives of these young people, that they shall be the better prepared to complete the tasks we shall be compelled to leave undone, I would urge that wherever it is practicable the various Grand Jurisdictions establish some form of Juvenile Department such as they have in Texas where they work under Charter and Ritual issued by the Grand Patron of that Jurisdiction, and that in those jurisdictions where such is not thought practicable, there be organized a Junior Division of the National Association for the Advancement of Colored People in which Race History is taught and black ideals instilled into our young people thus fitting them for the leadership of the next generation.

And while I would not suggest the taking of our Order into politics, yet in this new day our women everywhere should be urged to make use of their right of suffrage, where they are permitted to do so and that when they vote not to fail to place in office men and women who will safeguard the interest of our group as well as the public in general in both State and National Legislatures, and by so doing we may do away with the present status wherein our National Congress has failed for two sessions to pass the Dyer Anti-Lynching bill, because as the Senators themselves declare there has been no demand for such legislation on the part of their constituents.

UNION HALL—St. Paul, Minn.

During the biennial period, we have received and replied to many communications enquiring for suggestions as to how to adjust all kinds of perplexing problems, some of them arising out of a lack of co-operation between the Grand Matron and the Grand Patron, in most of which cases the Grand Patron has overlooked the fact that the Grand Matron is the presiding officer, and he her legal adviser or assistant, not her superior dictator; and to avoid a recurrence of such we would urge upon the brethren, should there be any such present, that they use more precaution in assuming the prerogatives of the presiding Grand Matron; that they spend a little more time studying the constitutions and laws of the Order that they may get a proper conception of the relative functions of the offices of Grand Matron and Grand Patron and that they not attempt to perform both.

But perhaps the most unfortunate difficulty that has come to our attention is that in several Jurisdictions the Grand Master of A.F. & A.M. seems to have conceived the idea that he is also Grand Master of the O.E.S. and has even gone so far as to carry his contentions in this respect into the civil courts, thus proving to the members of the other race either that our men have no confidence in their women or that we are not yet ready for our own leadership.

Now it is true that our Order was originated by Master Masons for the protection of their wives, widows, mothers, sisters and daughters and hence cannot exist without the co-operatnon of the members and more especially the officers of the Blue Lodges; and in my humble judgment it is conducive to the strength and growth of both the O.E.S. and the A.F. & A.M., that the most cordial co-operation should exist between these two organizations.

But in some Jurisdictions, notably in Missouri and the states of Washington, Louisiana and West Virginia instead of co-operation we have had the most bitter antagonism.

In each of these Jurisdictions, the Grand Lodge or its officers have gone so far as to organize an opposition Grand Chapter resulting in one side or the other appealing to the civil courts for protection in what they claim to be their rights in the matter.

But the civil courts are always slow to step in and attempt to arbitrate between two contending factions of fraternal or a religious organization, like Pilate when the Jews brought to him their accusations against the Savior which were purely religious, and he attempted to wash his hands clear of the whole matter, neither have the civil courts in either of these Jurisdictions made any ruling that would enable us to determine which of the rival Grand Chapters is the legal one.

In the state of Washington, however, as will be discovered by a careful reading of the "Final Order and Judgment" in the case a copy which was presented to us while on our visit to the Mt. Tacoma Grand Chapter, about the only thing the court did was to enjoin the Grand Master by himself or deputy from further suspending members of the A.F. & A.M. who were affiliated with the opposition Chapter, "except in good faith, after written charges have been preferred against them, and after trial in their respective lodges, in accordance with the procedure in such cases made and provided for in Masonic Laws."

So far as we have been advised there has been no final decision in the Missouri case, but it is not unreasonable to expect that the Missouri court, if it ever decides at all, will in all probability follow the example of the Washington and other courts thus leaving intact the two Grand Chapters in each of these Jurisdictions, each claiming to be the only legitimate one and accusing the other of being irregular or "clandestine," which is indeed an embarrassing situation, and such as ought not to exist; and while we realize that this International Conference is only a "conference," not having or claiming to have any authority to step in and decide which of these rival Grand Chapters is right; yet we do believe that since it is a "conference" of Grand Chapters it is the proper place for representatives of these rival Grand Chapters to come

1907   PAST MATRONS OF INTERNATIONAL CONFERENCE OF GRAND CHAPTERS O.E.S.   1924

MRS. LOTTIE ENGRAM, P.I.M.
(Illinois)
1907-1912

MRS. IVEY T. AXTON, P.I.M.
(Florida)
1912-1916

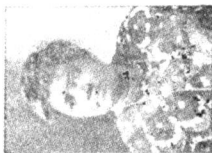

MISS ANNIE L. COX, P.I.M.
District of Columbia
1916-1920

MRS. FLORENCE L. SCOTT, P.I.M.
1920-1922

MRS. S. JOE BROWN, P.I.M.
(Iowa)
1922-1924

PANORAMIC VIEW OF INTERNATIONAL
GRAND MATRONS

PRINCE HALL   MASONIC TEMPLE
Boston, Mass.

together and confer and that it is our duty as representatives of sister Grand Jurisdictions to lend our influence and good offices to assist them if possible to settle their differences, which it seems the civil courts are unable or unwilling to do.

Hence believing that some good might be accomplished along this line by a free and open discussion here of the respective prerogatives of the Grand Lodges and Grand Chapters, I have given over an hour Friday morning at 10 o'clock to the discussion of the subject "Co-operation between the A.F. & A.M. and the O.E.S. in which discussion I have invited to participate a number of present and past Grand Masters including the two who are accused of overstepping their prerogatives in organizing rival Grand Chapters of O.E.S. in jurisdictions where regular Grand Chapters already existed.

We have also invited to be present and participate in this discussion, each of the male presiding officers of the other International Bodies that are holding sessions here at this time; and while some have already voiced their protest at our allowing the accused Grand Masters to be heard, we feel that they are nevertheless our brethren. We are their wives, mothers, sisters and daughters and believe that no harm and unquestionably much good might result from this symposium.

NECROLOGY

Since our last Biennial Session, the Grim Reaper has invaded our ranks and has robbed us of some of our brightest jewels.

It is therefore with deepest regret that we report the passing of Sis. Kittie Terrill, of St. Paul, Minn., a past Grand Matron of the Illinois Jurisdiction and the first Matron of this International Conference, and Sister Emma Kennedy, another past Grand Matron of Illinois, who was with us at our last Conference at which she was appointed our International Marshal.

On each of these occasions and on the ocassion of the passing of two other members of our Order, who were not members of this Conference, because of their wonderful contributions to the uplift of womanhood and the cause of humanity in general, we sent messages of condolence to the bereaved relatives, in the name of this Conference.

The other two sisters to whom I refer were Mrs. Nora F. Taylor, of Chicago, Grand Daughter Ruler of the National Grand Temple of Daughters of the I.B.P.O.E.W., and Mrs. Mary B. Talbert of Buffalo, N. Y., President of the Frederick Douglass Memorial and Historical Assn., Honoray President of the National Association of Colored Women and the only woman to whom has been awarded the Spingarn Medal of the N.A.A.C.P.

To assist in perpetuating the memory of Sister Kittie Terrill, Sis. Janie L. Cox and our other past International Matrons I have had made and brought with me to this Conference a panoramic portrait containing the likeness of each arranged in order and giving the name of each , the Grand Jurisdiction from which she hailed and the dates that she served you, to be sold at a nominal fee so as to cover the cost of the making of the cuts and the printing.

Having for several years filled the office of Foreign Correspondent of my own, the Iowa Jurisdiction, I find that there seems to be much confusion in the minds of some as to the duties of this office; I also find great differences of opinion relative to the manner of appointing and the duties of Foreign Representatives.

I also find that there is still much confusion in our various Grand Jurisdictions concerning the so-called "higher degrees."

Because of these misunderstandings, much time is consumed and the work of our beautiful Order very much muddled in some of the subordinate Chapters; and since as we have already suggested that one of the prime objects of this Conference is to try to aproach uniformity along all lines of O.E.S. work, we have placed on our program each of these topics for an open discussion, in which we hope to bring out the opinion of the best brains of the Order, which we are sure we have present here and we urge upon those among us of less ex-

PRINCE HALL MASONIC TEMPLE—Chicago, Ill.

MASONIC TEMPLE—Washington, D. C.

perience along these several lines to take the most
earnest heed to the opinions of those better informed than ourselves and when we return to our several Grand Jurisdictions, let us put into   practice
what shall here be agreed upon as the proper method of doing these things; for it is only   through
some such method as this that we shall ever arrive
at anything like uniformity of work.

   Those of us who were present or who have read
the proceedings of our last Biennial Session will
remember that at that session we were favored by
the presence and an address of Dr. Wm. Pickens,
one of the Field Secretaries of the National Association for the Advancement of Colored People
in response to which this conference adopted a stir-
ring resolution endorsing the work of the organization and urging upon the U. S. Senate the pas-
sage of the Dyer Anti-Lynching Bill; and pursuant
to the spirit of this resolution and in order to' place
our organization on record in a more tangible way
especially with reference to the Dyer Anti-Lynching Bill in October, 1922, with the co-operation
of the good women of our own state, we raised and
sent into the Anti-Lynching Fund of the N.A.A.C.
P. the sum of two hundred dollars, as a result of
which we were asked along with one hundred other
men and women of both races who had taken prom-
inent parts in this anti-lynching drive, to give a
brief statement for publication by the Anti-Lynching Committee, which we gave under the Caption
of "The International Conference of Grand Chapters of O.E.S."

   In the early part of the year 1923 we received a
communication from Mrs. Addie W. Hunton, another Field Secretary of the N.A.A.C.P., as Chairman of the Committee on Foreign Relations, inviting us to go as a representative of this Conference
to the Third Pan-African Conference which   was
held in London and other points in Europe, sug-
gesting that she was sure you would be pleased to
take care of the expense of something like a thous-
and dollars; and while I knew or rather believed
that you were desirous of being a factor in all worth
while movements especially for Racial uplift, I felt

that the time was not ripe for us to assume an obligation quite so great as this; hence I did not even take the matter up with my cabinet, but did send a message to the Conference bearing the greetings and best wishes of this International Body.

In Febraury 1924, I received a communication from Dr. Kelley Miller, inviting me as your presiding officer to participate in the Sanhedrin or All-Race conference to be held in Chicago the week of the 11th of that same month, and appreciating in a measure the importance of such a movement, having myself organized on Mar. 10, 1923 and Inter-Fraternal Council for my home-city, Des Moines, Ia., comprising representatives of a majority of the 33 subordinate fraternal organizations in that city coming from seven different fraternal families or institutions, having an object quite similar to that of the Sanhedrin, namely closer contact between different of our groups, without expense to this conference and with a view to giving further publicity to our organization, I delegated Sister Louisa U. Webb, our International Secretary, who resides in Chicago, to represent us in that meeting and to report the same to this conference.

My first official act after the close of our last Conference was to have printed fourteen hundred letterheads containing the names and addresses of all our International Officers and to issue an order on our International Treasurer in payment of the same.

I next sent a letter of greeting to each Grand Matron, apprising them of the achievements of our 8th Biennial Conference and inviting them to be present at this session, and followed these up with letters of greeting to the several Grand Chapters as they met, then by the questionnaires already referred to; these with my repeated attempts to get into touch with Grand Chapters of other continents and my responses to the innumberable communications that have come to this office during the biennium have necessitated my sending out several hundred communications in the interest of this Conference.

RECOMMENDATIONS

I recommend that in the interest of uni
formity, the Grand Matrons and Patrons here present pledge themselves that they will recommend
to their respective Grand Chapters, that hereafter
no degrees be conferred in our O.E.S. Chapters
except the five degrees of the Order of Eastern
Star, this of course having no reference to regularly organized and duly constituted Palaces of the
Queen of the South Courts of the Royal and exalted
Degree of Amaranth working under Chapters or
Warrants of Grand Bodies of these degrees.

In view of the fact that the Macoy Ritual which
is being used by most of the Grand Chapters of our
people throughout the United States and Canada,
is an exposed work, the sale of which is not con-
fined to members of the Order, I recommend that
this International Conference appoint a committee
to compile a ritual for our Order to be copyrighted
and published under the supervision of this Conference and to be sold only to those known to be members of our Order.

I also recommend that a committee be appointed
to publish a history of the Order of the Eastetrn
Star among Colored people, to be distributed at a
nominal price among our members and any others
who may be interested, for by this means, we shall
not only be preserving a most important phase of
our Race History but shall also attract to our
beautiful Order many who are ignorant of its
glorious record of achievements of both the present
and the past.

In conclusion permit me again to expres to you
my profound gratitude for having had the privilege
of serving you during the biennial period that is
now about to close; in the manifold duties of which
I have been greatly assisted by our very efficient
International Secretary to whom in particular and
to all my International cabinet in general I feel
deeply grateful, and while we have not been able
to accomplish all that we had hoped we might, we
have done our very best to live up to the resolution
we made upon our elevation to this most exalted
station, namely to show our appreciation by ren-
dering service to the cause.

YOUTH OR JUVENILE DEPARTMENT

The followng Jurisdictions have a Youth or Juvenile Department, Texas has 45 Chapters, Georgia 52 Chapters, and California's latest record shows 6 Chapters installed in 1923, while the number of Chapters is not given in latest Oklahoma report the record gives them a membership of 150, and while we have no record of number of Chapters or members in Ark. yet we find that they have also established this Department.

PRINCE HALL MASONIC AND O.E.S. HOME
Rockland Island, Ill.

HOMES AND TEMPLES

Woman has always been   known as a home-
builder, although the great world knows little of
her deeds of heroism, her self-denial and her real
devotion to suffering humanity. By experience she
knows what it is to be widowed and   homeless,
therefore she has gladly contributed   her part in
furnishing and supporting Homes for widows and
orphans, and has constantly urged the fraternity
to build such where there are none.

Our women as well as our men realize the importance   of having a meeting place in which to
carry on their activities in which to transact their
business and in which to hold heir Annual Communications; hence to this end they have used their
clever methods of raising funds, in buying bonds
and helpng to devise every possible mean of erecting and paying for Masonic Temples which wherever established   have proven not only a blessing
to the Masonic   family, but a credit to the com-
munity in which they were erected.

Of the three thousand and more Chapters dis-
persed about the globe either alone or   with   the
assistance of the A.F. & A.M. they have made mar-
velous progress along this line.

Many states like North Carolina, Arkansas, California and others with large Negro populations,
have Homes and Masonic Halls owned   by the
subordinate   lodges and chapters throughout   the
state, and in still others, like Iowa with but a mea-
ger Negro population, we find as many as four Masonic buildings although not spacious in their con-
structon, yet erected or purchased by the A.F. &
A.M. with the assistance of the O.E.S. While we
have been unable to secure the photo, we are informed that at Jacksonvlle, Fla. stands a Widows
and Orphan Home which is the joint property of
the Masons and the O.E.S. of that Jurisdiction and
is jointly mantained by these two organizations.

At Americus, Ga., we have a Masonic Orphanage, erected in 1898 by the Grand Lodge of A.F.
& A.M. with a boy's dormitory furnished at an ex-

pense of $14,000 contributed by the Grand Chapter of O.E.S. The inmates of this home which are taught Domestic Science and Agriculture. It has a campus of twenty-eight acres upon which practically all the food stuffs consumed in the Orphanage are raised.

Illinois Jurisdiction maintains a Home at Rock Island, known as Prince Hall Masonic and Eastern Star Home. It is valued at ten thousand dollars. The Masons and Eureka Grand Chapter O.E.S. jointly maintain the Home. It is all paid for and modernly improved. Have owned it ten years.

Eureka Grand Chapter O.E.S. owns property at Harvey, Illinois, worth three thousand dollars, all paid for and is simply a real estate investment which brings a revenue to the Grand Body.

In South Carolina the Masons purchased a building at Columbia which they remodeled into a most magnificant Masonic Temple. It is splendidly situated in one of the business centers of the city, just a few steps from Main Street and within three minutes walk from the Capitol. On the first floor are two large well appointed store rooms, on the second floor seven suits of rooms and a large assembly hall and on the third the lodge room. It is the home of both the Grand Lodge of A.F. & A.M. and the Grand Chapter of O.E.S.

Tennessee, the second oldest jurisdiction maintains at Nashville a Home for widows and orphans valued at $100,000 which home occupies a plot of thirty-seven acres upon which they raise much of the provisions consumed by the inmates of the Home.

The Grand Chapter of Indiana jointly with the Grand Lodge of this state own what they term a Masonic and Eastern Star Home, located in a beautiful grove about six miles east of Marion which they purchased October 22, 1921 for the sum of six thousand eight hundred fifty dollars and upon which they paid the last dollar on Sept. 9, 1922.

Union Hall, a Bldg. put up by the Union Hall Association at St. Paul, Minn. is among the first lodge halls built and owned by Negroes in the Northwest.

It is a brick building containing two full stories above the basement and is valued at $30,000. The basement contains a gymnasium, bowling alley, show booths and locker rooms; on the first floor there is a large assembly hall with checking room and offices; and, on the second floor lodge rooms in which meetings for both the Blue Lodges and the O.E.S are held.

At Birmingham, Alabama the Masons recently dedicated a Temple which cost $657,704. It contains a basement, an auditorium and galleries with seating capacity for 2000, also six store rooms, four lodge rooms and one hundred fifty-four office rooms.

The Birmingham Age Herald says: "Not only is this edifice a credit to that part of the city in which it is located because of its imposing appearance, but it represents thrift and enterprise on the part of those who made it possible." --

There are in this jurisdiction twelve hundred sixteen lodges and chapters with a membership of more than forty thousand.

Dr. A. Baxter Whitby, Grand Master of Masons of Oklahoma Jurisdiction has the following to say by way of appreciation of Oklahoma O.E.S.:

"Strikingly so, do we find recorded here and there in Masonic history the silent yet glowing achievements of our Noble Women of the Order of the Eastern Star and when the records of one Grand Lodge, that of St. John's of Oklahoma, are opened, tribute will be given to women of this our Jurisdiction.

We gladly give credit to the sound judgment and good common sense of the Masons of Oklahoma when they conceived the idea of erecting a Masonic Temple as a Home for the St. John's Grand Lodge of Negro Masons.

The idea was conceived, the plans determined upon and Boley, Oklahoma, a Negro town, the place of location.

With enthusiasm the work began with every prospect for completing the building in the appointed time.

However, it is not always ours to appoint the

time nor season. About 1912 the panic came, the overtaxed lodges weakened, many Masons became discouraged and fell by the wayside, murky darkness like a cloud overshadowed us, contractors threatened and at times seemed as if we would break in twain. Then it was that the Noble Order of the Eastern Star of Oklahoma with her 3000 women led by that brilliant enthusiastic and Christian woman, Mrs. Lillie Talliaferro, our present Grand Worthy Matron, came to the front, laid down upon the altar all of their many years' hoarding and said to Grand Master, G. I. Currin, "We bring you our all and pledge ourselves to help you to complete the work so worthy begun."

So it has gone from year to year, sometimes one, sometimes two and sometimes five thousand dollars at the time laid down as an offering from these worthy women until now we boast of a magnificent Temple worth eighty thousand dollars and all paid for, 140 by 50 feet, three stories high and all told a beautiful monument of brick and stone dedicated to the toil of the men and women of the Masnic Order of Oklahoma.

Walk into their brilliant Chapter room with me and you behold the handi-work of these same women. The most elaborate furnishings, altars, desks, pedestals, the finest of five pointed carpet and Stars and pedestals to match, and the walls decorated with emblems and columns with arch to crown all with their glory. Here in their beautiful sanctuary, the entire second floor dedicated to them alone and cherished so highly by all of us of St. John's, you find depicted here and there and yonder their skill in industry, art and song.

The industry is demonstrated in the beautiful quilts, pillow cases and fancy clothing made and exhibited from year to year by our young women in the state.

Their art display of needle work has taken honors at home and abroad and adorns the walls of the Chapter Room.

The whole is crowned with lovely music and song rendered from time to time by some of the most accomplished women of our State who glory in len-

MASONIC TEMPLE—Ft. Worth Texas

ding their bit and take pride in being enrolled as members. So let's lift our hats again, to our worthy women who with the other thousands throughout our Grand Organization in America send up their their voices in praises and cheer as we all go marching onward and upward and altogether love-ly.

At Fort Worth, Texas, the home of our present International Patron. is erected a modern three story brick Masonic Temple, which not only houses the Masonic Lodges and O.E.S. Chapters but also the headquarters of the official organ of the International Conference. The Eastern Star, you will also find in this Temple Fraternal Bank and Trust Co., a Negro financial institution with a capital of $100,000.

While in atendance upon the sessions of the eighth Biennial International Conference at Washigton, D.C. in August, 1922 we participated in the ceremonies acccmpanying the laying of the cornerstone of the magnificent Masonic Temple of that city which is the result of the joint efforts of the Masons and the members of the O.E.S.

In October 1924 the Grand Lodge of Illinois with appropriate ceremonies laid the corner stone of the new Prince Hall at the corner of 56th and Sta'e Streets in the financing of which the O.E.S. Chap-ters, courts of Heroine of Jericho and the Golden Circle as well as the various Masonic Lodges of Chicago are assisting; and when our 10th Biennial International Conference convenes in the city of Boston in Aug. 1926, the birth place of this or-ganization we shall in all probability be entertained at the new Prince Hall Masonic Temple, the property of Prince Hall Grand Lodge, the first Grand Lodge organized in America among colored men more than one hundred twenty-five years ago and in the same city where the first lodge was or-ganized among colored Masons with Prince Hall as Worshipful Master, in the fall of 1775. This temple is a five story modern brick structure built at a cost of $150,000, the last dollar of which was paid in February 1922.

REVISED CONSTITUTION AND BY-LAWS
OF THE
INTERNATIONAL CONFERENCE OF
GRAND CHAPTERS, O.E.S.

PREAMBLE

Whereas it has been clearly demonstrataed that there is necessity for the uniformity of the interpretation of the Ritualistic work of the Order of the Eastern Star in the several Jurisdictions of the Order, and a demand for a closer fraternal relationship among the various Grand Chapters and members of the Order in general, and as there is no supreme body in existance to which the Grand Jurisdictions hold allegiance, we the several Grand Chapters of the Order of the Eastern Star do hereby form ourselves into an organization the purpose of which shall be to strengthen the Fraternal chain and endeavor to bring out a uniformity of the Ritualistic work of the Order, bearing in mind, that the organization does not assume unto itself in any manner to exercise Jurisdiction over, or assume any powers of the respective Grand Chapters comprising this organization.

In order to make the foregoing object of the organization effective, we hereby promulgate the following Constitution and By-Laws.

ARTICLE I—NAME

This organization shall be known as and styled, the "International Conference of Grand Chapters of the Order of the Eastern Star."

ARTICLE II—MEMBERSHIP

Sec. 1. The membership of this Conference shall consist of the officers and past officers of the Conference; all present and Past Grand Worthy Matrons and Grand Worthy Patrons in attendance, of Jurisdictions affiliated in the Conference, together with the past Worthy Matrons of the Subordinate Chapters of the respective Jurisdictions, whose Grand Chapters affiliate in this conference.

MASONIC TEMPLE—Birmingham. Alabama

All past Grand Worthy Matrons and past Grand Worthy Patrons of the International Conference, in good standing in the Order of the Eastern Star, shall be "life members" of the Conference, endowed with all the honors within the gift of the Conference.

Sec. 2. Officers—The elective officers of the Conference shall be as follows:

International Grand Worthy Matron; International Grand Worthy Patron; International Grand Associate Matron; International Grand Associate Patron; International Grand Treasurer; International Grand Secretary; International Grand Conductress; International Grand Associate Conductress.

Sec. 3. The appointive officers of the Conference shall be as follows:

International Grand Adah; International Grand Ruth; International Grand Esther; International Grand Martha; International Grand Electa; International Grand Lecturer; International Grand Warder; International Grand Sentinel; International Grand Chaplain; International Grand Organist; International Grand Marshall in the East; International Grand Marshall in the West; Chairman of the Committee on Foreign Correspondence; Chairman on Jurisprudence; Chairman Committee on Finance.

Sec. 4. The foregoing officers shall be elected, appointed and installed at each Biennial Session of the International Conference of Grand Chapters of the Order of the Eastern Star, and shall hold their office until the next Biennial Session or until their successors are duly elected, appointed and installed, unless he or she shall fail to remain in good standing in their respective Grand Chapters.

ARTICLE III—MEETINGS

Sec. 1. The International Conference of Grand Chapters shall convene in Biennial Session at the same time and in the same city as the Grand Masters Council.

Sec. 2. All meetings shall be opened and closed in the Adoptive Rite or Eastern Star degree; and all business of the Conference shall be transacted in the Eastern Star degree and styled Conference.

This Conference shall not in any manner attempt to diminish or extend any of the powers invested or exercise by Grand Chapters affiliated in the Conference; nor shall any law be created that may effect in a compulsory manner, members of Subordinate or Grand Chapters.

It shall be the effort of the Conference to benefit the Jurisdictions by submitting to them for their own consideration, through their representatives, recommendations, which may be conductive to a uniformity of the ritualistic work of the Order of the Eastern Star throughout our Jurisdictions.

Sec. 3. Votes—Each Jurisdiction affiliated in the Conference shall have three votes on every subject, to be cast by the legally elected representative which shall be the Worthy Grand Matron, Grand Patron or their proxies duly authorized by the Jurisdictions and holding credentials of their Grand Chapters duly signed by the Grand Secretary of said Grand Jurisdiction authenticated by the seal of the Grand Chapter represented.

Sec. 4. The present Grand Officers of the Conference who shall have been duly elected, appointed and installed shall each have one vote on every question.

Sec. 5. The other voters shall consit of the Past Grand Worthy Matrons and Patrons of the several Grand Jurisdictions holding membership in the Conference, who shall have one vote each on all questions except the election of officers of the Conference.

Sec. 6. The voting for election of officers shall be by Jurisdictions and the votes shall be cast as follows: Each Jurisdiction represented shall have three votes two of which shall be cast by the legally elected representatives of their duly authorized proxies; and one vote to be divided among the Past Grand Worthy Matrons and Past Grand Worthy Patrons of the Jurisdictions represented.

Each present grand officer of the Conference and chairman of standing committees shall have one vote, provided however, that no member shall be allowed to vote in more than one capacity.

Sec. 7. All present and past Grand Worthy Matrons and Worthy Patrons of the International Conference in attendance of Jurisdictions affiliated in the Conference are eligible to election or appointment to any office within the gift of the International Conference.

ARTICLE IV—REVENUE

Sec. 1. In order to defray the expenses of the Conference and other necessary expenses connected therewith, each Jurisdiction affiliated in the Conference shall contribute biennially the sum of one cent for each member under its Jurisdiction.

BY-LAWS
ARTICLE I—DUTIES OF OFFICERS

Sec. 1. It shall be the duty of the International Grand Matron of the International Conference to open, preside over and close the International Coference at each biennial session. To appoint all committees, unless otherwise provided for, appoint all appointive officers; decide all questions submitted to her; inspect and sign all drafts drawn on the Treasurer. She shall make a report to the Conference of all her official acts at each biennial session.

Sec. 2. It shall be the duty of the International Grand Patron, to assist and advise the International Grand Matron in the discharge of her duties; and in the absence of the Grand Matron and the Associate Grand Matron, he shall discharge all the duties designated for the International Grand Matron.

Sec. 3. The International Associate Grand Matron shall in the event of the death, absence or disability of the Grand Matron, assume and perform all the duties of the International Grand Matron.

Sec. 4. In the event of the death, absence or disability of the International Patron, the International Associate Grand Patron shall perform all the duties of the International Grand Patron.

Sec. 5. The International Grand Treasurer shall keep an accurate account of all receipts and expenditures of all moneys, carefully number and file all vouchers; and make a written statement at each biennial session of the Conference, reporting the receipts, expenditures and balance of money on hand, submitting at the same time the books, receipts, and vouchers for examination by the International Grand Matron and Committee appointed to audit the same.

After the election and qualification of the Treasurer-elect, the retiring Treasurer shall deliver to her successor in office all books, vouchers, receipts and other property in her possession belonging to the Conefrence.

Sec. 6. The other officers shall perform the duties of officers filling relative office s in their Grand Chapters of the O.E.S.

ARTICLE II—STANDING   COMMITTEES

Immediately after the installation   of   the officers of the International Confdrence, the Grand Worthy Matron of the Conference shall apoint the following standing committees,   consisting of five members each, the chairman of each which shall be considered an officer of the International Conference, namely: Committee on Foreign Correspondence, whose duty shall be to perform the usual duties required in the spread of the Order in the various Jurisdictions; Committee on Jurisprudence, whose duty it shall be to examine and report upon all decisions of the presiding officers of the International Conference and all questions of law, that may be referred to them by the presiding officers of the Conference, to examine all propositions, to amend or repeal any provision of the Constitution, By-Laws, Rules and Regulations of the Conference or of the Order, and report its findings with recommendations to the Conference or to the Presiding Officer as the case may require.

Committee on Finance, whose duty it shall be to examine and pass on all bills presented to the Conference and report to the Conference an estimate of the amount to be appropriated to pay the expenses of the Conference; and no appropriaton shall be made until passed upon and recommended by the Finance Committee. To examine the books,

WIDOWS' AND ORPHANS' HOME
Nashville, Tennessee

records and vouchers of the Treasurer and Secretary and report thereon with a stated detail of the financial affairs of the International Conference.

ARTICLE III—SESSION COMMITTEES

Sec. 1. At each session of the International Conference, immediately after the opening of the Conference, the Grand Matron shall appoint the following committees and such other as she may deem necessary to assist during the sessions, consisting of five members each, namely; Committee on Credentials, whose duty it shall be to carefully examine the credentials of all persons claiming the right of membership and vote and report their names and Jurisdictions they hail from to the Conference; to properly list the names of all officers of the Conference and all representatives and proxies of the various Grand Jurisdictions affiliated in the Conference.

Committee to examine all visiting members of the Order present and report on those who are not properly vouched for.

ARTICLE IV—RULES OF ORDER

Sec. 1. There shall be a program arranged for each biennial session of the Conference, under the special direction of the International Grand Matron, of the Conference or a committee appointed by her. The program shall contain the order of business and subjects of papers to be read and discussed during the session.

Sec. 2. All business and reports shall be disposed of before the Conference is closed except such as may by two-thirds vote lie over until the next Biennial Session.

Sec. 3. No member shall speak more than twice upon a subject except by the unanimous consent of the Conference.

Sec. 4. All resolutions, propositons or other matters requiring the action of the Conference shall be presented in writing, signed by the author, to the conference, the first two days, in order that they may be referred to the proper committee, for its consideration, in order that the committee may

examine the   items   placed in their hands, offer
recommendations thereon and report on the same
before action is taken, by the conference.

Sec. 5. "Robert's Rules of Order"   shall be the
paliamentary guide in all cases not ctherwise provided for.

STATISTICAL REPORT

JURISDICTIONS	CHAPTERS	MEMBERS
Arkansas	325	9750
Arizona	6	161
Alabama	429	10000
California	27	1115
Colorado	12	500
District of Columbia	10	2800
Delaware		500
Florida	68	2500
Georgia	435	18000
Iowa	26	1000
Illinois	94	5500
Indiana	48	1746
Kansas	85	2590
Kentucky	86	3054
Liberia		
Louisaina	84	527
Maryland	33 --	1123
Michigan	23	1200
Mississippi		11630
Missouuri (Harmony)	27	2835
Missouri (United)	21	370
New England	17	790
New Jersey	28	1014
New York	41	2200
Nebraska	9	500
North Carolina	466	11400
Ohio	58	1101
Oklahoma	155	3500
Ontario	6	199
Pennsylvania	48	1900
South Carolina	31	2279
Tennesse	240	5000
Texas	233	6000
Virginia	71	3000
Washington (Mt. Tacoma)	6	347
West Virginia (Sovereign)	35	1690
West Virginia (Prince Hall)		300
	3,434	**120,101**

GRAND CHAPTERS IN ORDER OF THEIR ORGANIZATINON

The following is a list cf Grand Chapters in the order of their Seniority, the numbers prefixed being of existing Chapters:

1. North Carolina, September	1880
2. Tennessee, June	1881
3. California, December	1882
4. Kansas, August	1883
5. Louisaina (No. 1.), June 30	1884
6. Kentucky, August	1885
7. Arkansas, July 12	1886
8. Ohic, August 3	_1887
9. Indiana, October 25	1888
10. Michigan, August 21	1889
11. Texas, January 20	1890
12. Illinois, August 11	1890
13. Missouri (No. 1), December	1890
14. Dis.rict of Columbia, May 24	1892
15. Ontario, April	1894
16. Alabama, June 21	1894
17. New England, November 3	1894
18. Mississippi	1894
19. New Yark, October 18	1895
20. Maryland, November	1896
21. Georgia, June 3	1898
22. Oklahoma, August 9	1898
23. Liberia, January 24	1903
24. Virginia, July 26	1903
25. Iowa, May 21	1907
Supreme G. C., August	1907
26. South Carolina, July 10	1908
27. Pennsylvania, November	1909
28. New Jersey, June 24	1913
29. West Virginia, June	1913
30. Washington (No. 1), July	1913
31. West Virginia (No. 2), July 16	1914
32. Arizona, July 11	1921
33. Nebraska, Octcber 15	1921
34. Missouri (No. 2), October 27	1921
35. Colorado, July 24	1922
36. Florida (Date unknown)	
37. Delaware (Date unknown)	
38. Washington (No. 2.) (Date unknown)	

PRINCE HALL MASONIC TEMPLE—
New York City, N. Y.

ANNUAL COMMUNICATIONS

District of Columbia _ __ __ _____January
Liberia _ __ __ ___ ____ ____ _____ January
Florida __ __ _____ _____ _____ _____April
Arizona __ __ _ _____ ____ _____ ____ May
California _____ ____ __ ____ _____ __June
Indiana ____ ___ __ ____ ____ ____ __ ____June
New Jersey ____ ____ ____ ____ ___ _____June
Missouri (No. 1) ___ _____ _____ _____ June
Louisiana _____ ____ ____ ____ _ _____June
New York _____ ____ ___ _____ __ _____June
Iowa __ _ __ ____ _____ ____ ____ ___ __June
West Virginia (No. 1) ___ _____ ____ __June
West Virginia (No. 2)_ __ _ ____ _____June
Virginia ___ ___ _____ ____ __ _____ July
Pennsylvania _____ __ _____ ____ _____July
Arkansas ____ ___ _____ _____ __ _July
South Carolina _ _____ _____ ____July
Washington (No.1) __ _____ ____ _____ __July
Washington (No. 2)___ ___ _____ _____July
Texas _____ ___ _____ _____ ___ ___ ____July
Mississippi __ _____ _____ ____ ____July
Colorado __ _____ _____ _____August
Tennessee ___ _____ ___ _____ _____August
Ohio ___ _____ __ ____ ___ ____August
Illinois __ __ __ ____ _____ ____ _____August
Oklahoma _ _____ ____ _____ ___ ____ _August
Kansas __ _____ _____ _____ __ August
Kentucky___ _____ _____ _____ ___ ___August
Alabama _ . _____ _____ __ _____ August
Georgia ____ ___ ____ _____ ____ __ ____August
Ontario __ _____ _____ _____ ____ __August
North Carolina _____ __ _____ ___September
New England _____ _____ _____ September
Michigan _____ _____ _____ ____ __October
Nebraska _____ _____ _____ ___October
Missouri (No. 2) _____October
Maryland _____ ___ __ __ _____ ____November

GRAND CHAPTER DIRECTORY

Arkansas—Grand Matron, Mrs. M. J. Johnson
    Box 94, Arkansas City,
    Grand Patron—H. W. Wheeler
    Box 52, Gum Springs
Arizona—Grand Matron, Mrs. Lynn Ross Carter
    714 Grant St., Phoenix
    Grand Patron—Clay Credille

    1321 E. Madison St., Pheonix
Alabama—Grand Matron, Mrs. Janie Blasco
    152 Lyon St., Mobile   __
    Grand Patron—I. H. Rose
    Box 16, Wetumpka
California—Grand Matron, Mrs. Aline J. Hueston
    1729 Forest St., Bakersfield
    Grand Patron—J. G. Edmonds
    1360 E. 33rd St., Los Angeles
Colorada—Grand Matron, Mrs. Mary G. Clinkscale
    2508 Fremont Place, Denver
    Grand Patron—Samuel N. Nelson
    107 South Union , Pueblo
Dist. of Columbia—Grand Matron, Mrs. Annie M.
    Gray, 628 L St.N. E., Washington
    Grand Patron—Samuel T. Craig
    1646½ N. J. Ave. N. W. Washington
Delaware—Grand Matron, Mrs. Eliza Colbert
    410 Taylor St., Wilmington
Florida—Grand Matron, Mrs. Inez T. Alston
    1611 Lamar Ave., Tampa
    Grand Patron—Dr. J. M. Wise, Tallahasse
Georgia—Grand Matron, Mrs. Viola E. Felton
    Americus
    Grand Patron—Sol. C. Johnson, Savannah
Iowa—Grand Matron, Mrs .Eva L. Abbey   __
    414 E. 25th, Minneapolis, Minnesota
    Grand Patron—Rev. E. R. Edwards, Ottumwa
Illinois—Grand Matron, Mrs. Carrie Lee Hamilton
    Mounds
    Grand Patron—A. B. Dawson, Rock Island
Indiana—Grand Matron, Mrs. Mamie J. Russell
    32 Noble St., Wabash
    Grand Patron—John C. Dawson.
    434 N. West St., Indianapolis

Kansas—Grand Matron, Mrs. Lulu M. Gudgell
    720 E. Morena Ave., Colorado Springs, Colo.
Grand Patron—C. B. Walker, Chetopa, Kan.
Kentucky—Grand Matron, Mrs. Sarah E. Peppers
    Box 214, Lexington
Grand Patron—Jas. L. Dunlap
    108 S. Atkinson Ave., Earlington
Louisiana—Grand Matron, Mrs. A. A. Edwards
    1738 Constantinople St., New Orleans
Liberia—Grand Matron, Mrs. Izetta C. Stevens
    Monrovia
Maryland—Grand Matron, Mrs. Alice R. Dansbury
    506 Somerset St., Baltimore
Grand Patron—Patrick M. Turner
    1621 Miller St., Baltimore
Michigan—Grand Matron, Mrs. Mable G. Harrison
    115 E. 6th St., Flint
Grand Patron—Wm. R. Evans, Detroit
Missouri (Harmony)—Grand Matron, Mrs. Alma A.
    Clark, 2814 St. Louis Ave., St. Louis
Grand Patron—M. W. Wilson
    2454 Flora Ave., Kansas City
Missouri (United)—Grand Matron, Mrs.   Marie
    Hedgemon, 2844 St. Louis Ave., St. Louis
Grand Patron—Robert P. Jackson
    395 Farmington Avenue   St. Paul, Minn.
Mississippi—
New England—Grand Matron, Mrs.   Annie Eichel-
    berger, 64 Sawyer St., Boston, Mass.
Grand Patron—Thomas Coleman, New London
    Conn.
New Jersey—Grand Matron, Mrs. Lennie B. Hud-
    son, 614 N. Michigan Ave., Atlantic City
Grand Patron—Pearl Walden
    222 Delaware Ave., Jersey City
New York—Grand Matron, Mrs. Alice Campbell
    2291—7th Ave., New York City
Grand Patron—James E. Mason, Buffalo
Nebraska—Grand Matron, Mrs. Kate S. Wilson
    521 W. 33rd St., Omaha
Grand Patron—Nat'l Hunter
    2021 N. 28th St., Omaha
North Carolina—Grand Matron, Mrs. Sallie Evans
    619 Orange St., Fayetteville
Grand Patron—Dr. J. E. Shepard, Durham

Ohio—Grand Matron, Miss Ida M. Williams
111 N. 9th St., Columbus
Grand Patron—J. H. Weaver, Cleveland

Ontario—Grand Matron, Mrs. Lizzie Monroe
530 Windsor Ave., Windsor
Grand Patron—W. F. Brown
2329 18th St., Detroit, Michigan

Oklahoma—Grand Matron, Mrs. Lillie Talliaferro
406 6th St., Perry
Grand Patron—W. L. Waid
703 N. 5th St., Muskogee

Pennsylvania—Grand Matron, Mrs. A. E. W. Gold-
sten, 2126 Heman St., Pittsburgh
Grand Patron—W. L. Winston
1411 N. 3rd St., Harrisburgh

South Carolina—Grand Matron, Mrs. R. H. Walton
Columbia
Grand Patron—E. J. Sawyer, Bennettsville

Tennessee—Grand Matron, Mrs. Ada C. La Prade
910 E. 3rd St., Chattanooga
Grand Patron—C. D. Hayes
Box 248, Arlington

Texas—Grand Matron, Mrs. C. H. Ellis
912 Crockett St., San Antonio
Grand Patron—J. C. Scott
401½ E. 9th St., Ft. Worth

Virginia—Grand Matron, Mrs. Essie C. Williams
723 Caledonia St., Portsmouth
Grand Patron—W. H. Jones
728 W. Marshall St., Richmond

Washington (Mt. Tacoma)—Grand Matron, Mrs.
Etta Hawkins, 743 Summit Ave., N. Seattle

Washington (Golden West)—Grand Matron, Mrs.
Nina Porter, 1508 E. Garland Ave., Spokane

West Virginia (Sovereign)—Grand Matron, Mrs.
Gertrude Brown, 913 Cornwal St., Parkersburg
Grand Patron—Rev. B. S. Dent   ·
P.O. Box 98, Thorpe

West Virginia (Prince Hall)—Grand Matron, Mrs.
Mary Harris, Mincar
Grand Patron—Shirley Waid, Wheeling

MASONIC TEMPLE—Columbus, South **Carolina**

PAST OFFICERS
OF
INTERNATIONAL GRAND CHAPTERS
O·E.S.
1907—1912

Mrs. Kittie Terrell _____ Grand Matron
          Illinois Jurisdiction
Walden Banks _____Grand Patron
          New England Jurisdiction
1912—1916
Mrs. Inez T. Alston _____Grand Matron
          Florida Jurisdiction
Dr. W. H. Jernagin_____Grand Patron
          Oklahoma Jurisdiction
1916—1920
Miss Janie L. Cox_____Grand Matron
          District of Columbia
Rev. J. H. Garrison_____Grand Patron
          Iowa Jurisdiction
1920—1922
Mrs. Florence E. Scott _____Grand Matron
          Ohio Jurisdiction
Wm. A. Baltimore_____ Grand Patron
          District of Columbia Jurisdiction
1922—1924
Mrs. S. Joe Brown _____Grand Matron
          Iowa Jurisdiction
Wm. A. Baltimore _____Grand Patron

OFFICERS OF THE
INTERNATIONAL CONFERENCE OF GRAND
CHAPTERS ORDER OF THE EASTERN
STAR
1924—1926

Mrs. S. Joe Brown, Worthy Matron
  1058 Fifth Avenue, Des Moines, Iowa
J. C. Scott, Worthy Patron
  401½ Ninth Street, Ft. Worth, Texas
Mrs. Ada C .La Prade, Associate Matron
  910 East Third St., Chattanooga, Tenn.
W. L. Waid, Associate Patron
  703 North Fifteenth St., Muskogee, Okla.
Mrs. Viola E. Felton, Treasurer
  520 West College, Americus, Ga.
Mrs. Louisa U. Webb, Secretary
  3807 Vincennes Ave., Chicago, Ill.
Mrs. Rosa J. Richardson, Conductress
  1119 Druid Hill Ave., Baltimore, Md.
Mrs. Marie Soanes, Associate Conductress
  2006 North Sixth St., Kansas City, Kansas
Mrs. Lillie Talliaferro, Chairman Finance
  Perry, Oklahoma
Mrs. L. R. Palmer Berry
  4938 Dearborn St., Chicago, Illinois
Mrs. Inez T. Alston, Lecturer
  Tampa, Florida
Mrs. E. E. Burnette, Editor "Eastern Star"
  Cleburne, Texas
Mrs. Marie L. Johnson, Adah. Washington, D.C.
Mrs. Mollie Williams, Ruth, Louisville, Ky.
Mrs. Kathryn Wilson, Esther, Omaha, Neb.
Mrs. Annabel Cooper, Martha, Providence. R. I.
Mrs. Mabel G. Harrison, Electa, Flint, Michigan
Mrs. Alice Campbell, Warder, New York City
Mrs. Sallie Evans, Sentinel, Fayetteville, N. C.
Mrs. Etta Hawkins, Marshal, West, Seattle, Wash.
Mrs. Prudence Penn, Marshal, East, Phila., Pa.
Mrs. Ida R. Harris, Chaplain, Petersburg, Va.
Rev. S. T. Craig, Jurisprudence Committee,
  Washington, D. C.

Mrs. Lynn Ross Carter, Deputy, Pacific Coast,
   714 W. Grant St., Pheonix, Ariz.
Mrs. Elizabeth Monroe, Deputy, Canada,
   530 Windsor Ave., Windsor, Ontario

BIENNIAL MEETINGS
INTERNATIONAL CONFERENCE
OF
GRAND CHAPTERS
O.E.S.

Boston, Mass. _____ 1907
Chicago, Ill. _____ 1908
Detroit, Mich. _____ 1910
Washington, D. C. _____1912
Pittsburgh, Pa. _____ 1914
Chicago, Ill. _____ 1916
Cincinnati, Ohio _____ 1920
Washington D.C. _____ 1922
Pitsburgh, Pa. _____ 1924
Boston, Mass. _____ 1926

"Go, History of the Eastern Star,
Where e'er its wandering children are:

Recall to those who hailed its birth
Their toilsome struggle 'mid the dearth
Of cheering words, or sunny ways;
And tell those of later days

How great the triumph it has met—
Lest they forget—lest they forget.
Now in these days of proud progress,
Forgot not those of storm and stress,

Encourage the same zeal and truth
Which marked our Order in its youth,
And let the future years reveal
The same desire for its best weal;

Then shall its record grow and blaze
With the refulgence of its rays,
Till earth, illumined, near and far
Reflects the light of Bethlehem's Star."

THE BYSTANDER PRESS

Des Moines, Iowa.